THE LITTLE BOOK OF
LAGOM

Andrews McMeel Publishing
a division of Andrews McMeel Universal
1130 Walnut Street, Kansas City, Missouri 64106

www.andrewsmcmeel.com

First published in 2017 by Summersdale Publishers Ltd., 46 West Street,
Chichester, West Sussex
PO19 1RP, UK.

18 19 20 21 22 SDB 10 9 8 7 6 5 4 3 2 1

ISBN: 978-1-4494-9115-4

Library of Congress Control Number: 2017947517

Photo research: Anna Martin
Editor: Jean Z. Lucas
Art Director: Julie Barnes
Production Manager: Tamara Haus
Production Editor: Maureen Sullivan

ATTENTION: SCHOOLS AND BUSINESSES
Andrews McMeel books are available at quantity discounts with bulk purchase for
educational, business, or sales promotional use. For information, please e-mail the
Andrews McMeel Publishing Special Sales Department: specialsales@amuniversal.com.

How to Balance Your
Life the Swedish Way

THE LITTLE BOOK OF
LAGOM

JONNY JACKSON
& ELIAS LARSEN

Andrews McMeel
PUBLISHING®

Contents

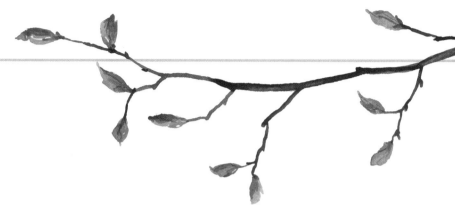

The *Lagom* Garden

What is lagom?

IS IT JUST *HYGGE* IN DISGUISE?

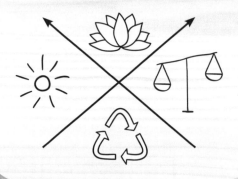

Hygge was the buzzword for 2016, and the fact that *lagom* is another Scandinavian concept which has made its way into our vocabulary is bound to make you wonder if they're similar, or even the same. The Danish art of *hygge* is about savoring simple daily pleasures and enjoying moments of calm, whereas the Swedish *lagom* (pronounced *lah-gom*) is a lifestyle choice with balance, modesty, unfussiness, and contentment at its heart. *Lagom* is a Swedish word meaning "just the right amount" and comes from the proverb *"Lagom är bäst,"* meaning "Just the right amount is best." *Lagom* can be worked into every aspect of your life, such as being more mindful of the amount of non-sustainable resources that you use;

managing a healthy diet and considering the carbon footprint of the products in your home; creating a work/life balance that's right for you; saving instead of spending; and thinking about the wider world and your impact upon it.

Lagom may sound like an exercise in frugality but in essence it's about living and enjoying a simpler life so that you focus on what's important. It's something that can be tailored to your individual needs with small tweaks to every aspect of your lifestyle to bring balance. Above all, you can be as *lagom* as you want to be, as it's not about everything being perfect; it's about being "just right" for you.

The origins of the word '*lagom*'

It's believed to derive from the phrase *"laget om,"* "around the team," which was used by the Vikings when passing around the communal libation in a horned vessel to ensure that everyone received their fair share.

PART 1

The Lagom Home

Ask yourself: Is it too much, not enough, or just the right amount?

There are many ways to be more *lagom* at home. This section offers opportunities, ideas, and inspiration on how to reduce your energy expenditure — such as tips for identifying and reducing drafts, how to reduce food waste, tips on growing your own produce, a guide on how to buy responsibly and sustainably — as well as some innovative ways to declutter, recycle, reuse, and upcycle.

Quick and easy ways to save energy around the home

It's not just roof insulation and double-pane windows that lower the heating bills. Here are some simple ways to save money on your energy bills:

- If you have wood floors, use area rugs to stop heat from escaping and to reduce drafts. They make the place look cozy, too.

- Turn down the heat overnight and invest in a thicker quilt or duvet for winter.

- Turn down your thermostat by one degree — this can create substantial savings on your fuel bills over the year.

- Make draft stoppers to reduce drafts under doors around the house. If you have old-style windows, make draft stoppers for these, too.

- Do you really need to wash your shirt after one wear? Air it out — hang it up on a hanger — and wear it for another day before throwing it in the wash.

- Ditch the tumble dryer — it's one of the biggest energy guzzlers in the home. Instead, dry your clothes outside or on a hanging rack indoors. Laundry smells so much better when it has been dried outdoors.

- Use blinds and curtains on windows to boost insulation and keep warmth in.

- Have a bundle of throws to cozy up with on TV nights instead of turning up the thermostat.

Switch to LED light bulbs in your home. Lighting accounts for around 18 percent of your electricity bill. LEDs use 85 percent less energy than traditional incandescent bulbs, and the light is the same.

Use rechargeable batteries — these use 23 times less nonreusable energy than single-use batteries.

Keep the oven door shut when it's on — up to a quarter of the heat escapes every time you open the oven door.

Turn off lights when you leave a room — so simple!

Have an induction cooktop installed — these are highly energy efficient as they direct the heat to the cookware and take minimal time to heat up.

- Avoid the dreaded "vampire power" — if your appliances are left on standby, they are leeching energy for no purpose. It's believed this "vampire power" can amount to between 5 and 10 percent of home energy use.

- Stop using paper towels and use clothes that can be washed and reused instead. Old T-shirts and bald towels make ideal soft cloths.

- Wash clothes in a cool wash or cold water — up to 90 percent of energy used by your washing machine is used to heat up the water. If you're worried that cold water won't keep your clothes as clean as a hot wash, there are a number of eco-friendly detergents that are formulated to work well when used with cold water.

Have nothing in your house that you do not know to be useful or believe to be beautiful.

WILLIAM MORRIS

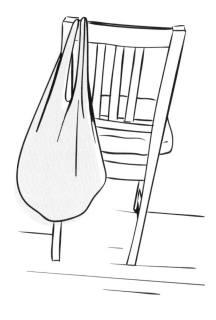

From T-shirt to tote bag

With just a few strategic snips, you can make a stylish, not to mention economical and eco-friendly, tote bag out of an old T-shirt. Let's be honest, recycled is far more desirable than a plastic alternative!*

You will need:

Cotton T-shirt

Scissors

Ruler

- Select a T-shirt. If it's not yours, ask first!

- Place the T-shirt flat on a work surface and cut off the sleeves along the shoulder seams.

- Turn the T-shirt inside out and place it on the work surface with the bottom seam closest to you. Arrange the bottom edges so they overlap neatly and cut vertical slits from the bottom all the way along, cutting about 2 inches deep and 1 inch apart. You can use a ruler to keep your cuts even.

- Next make a vertical cut along each side seam, also around 2 inches deep.

- Working from one side to the other, knot each set of cuts together. Double knot to create a secure base for your bag.

- Turn your new tote bag right side out, and it's ready to use.

* Of course there are many other uses for an old T-shirt, such as dust cloths, rag rugs, beanbags, and baby hats.

The wonderful versatility
of packing crates and pallets

People are quick to discard packing crates, but they are fantastically versatile. Check out these cheap and simple projects for the home — and they won't take more than an hour to make.

◁ DESK ORGANIZER

Attach a pallet to the wall above your desk and you have an instant desk organizer. If you're feeling artistic, give it a coat of paint, or leave as it is if you prefer the rustic look. Use the horizontal supports as shelving for inspirational images, plants, or pen cups.

SIDE TABLE ▷

A fruit crate makes a lovely scandi-look side table, especially if you give it a touch of paint — we love the whitewashed look.

FUNKY SHOE STORAGE ▷

For a statement shoe organizer that your children will enjoy using, place a wooden pallet on its side, attach it securely to the wall, and then invite your children to slide their shoes through the holes! Each child could have their own rack according to their height, so the tallest can have the top slot, etc.

RUSTIC ▷ STORAGE

Wooden crates balanced on top of each other make excellent and attractive storage. These can be picked up at your local craft or discount store.

Clean your home with homemade citrus cleaner

Store-bought cleaning products have a dizzying amount of ingredients. They're also expensive, and some are harmful to the environment, pets, and us, so instead of using them, make your own citrus vinegar cleaner. It's cheap, effective, and doubles as an insect repellant with its fresh, zesty aroma.

You will need:

1 (34-ounce) (approx.) glass container with a lid

4 cups white wine vinegar

Peel of two lemons and one lime (perhaps have that gin and tonic first or make lemonade)

1 spray bottle

Instructions:

- Fill the container with the white wine vinegar and add the lemon and lime peel.

- Leave the filled container to stand in a cool, dark place for a week or two until the vinegar becomes cloudy and the smell isn't so pungent.

- Transfer some of the solution into a spray bottle and then it's ready to use on floors, surfaces, and in bathrooms, wherever you would normally use spray cleaning products.

Super-duper draft stopper

Drafts under doors make for a chilly home as well as being costly when the heating bill arrives. Making homemade draft stoppers are the ideal way to stop drafts from coming in.

You will need:

- A rectangular piece of material, at least 15¾ inches wide and just 1½ inches longer than the width of the door (or you can use an old pair of pants and chop off a leg — in this case, skip to the fifth bullet in the list)
- Sewing machine or needle and thread
- A pair of thick tights
- Stuffing (beanbag filling is best, or rice, but you could even use tightly packed newspaper torn into strips)
- Pins

Instructions:

- Once you have cut your piece of material, iron it.
- Fold it lengthways so the design (if there is one) is on the inside.
- Pin the fabric together along the long edge and one of the ends ready for sewing.
- Stitch the fabric along the length of the long edge, then along just one of the ends. Then turn the fabric inside out so that you have a tube of fabric that is open at one end.
- Cut a leg off your tights and fill it with stuffing. When it's full and just a little bit smaller than your draft stopper, tie a knot in the end.
- Insert the stuffed tight into your draft stopper and stitch the other end closed.
- It's now ready to keep those drafts out!

Rag rug

Making a rag rug is a wonderful way of using up old fabric, such as towels, sheets, and clothing. T-shirts and towels make the softest rag rugs, but there is something special about using old clothes worn by you and/or family members that perhaps no longer fit or are beyond repair: You're literally weaving memories into the rug, which you can be reminded of every time you use it. It also serves as a stylish way to reduce drafts on bare floorboards.

You will need:

Old fabric

Canvas with ½-inch grid width, cut to the size that you want for your rag rug

Fabric scissors

Nimble fingers (!)

Instructions:

- Use the fabric scissors to snip the edge of the fabric at 2-inch intervals to make it easier to tear. Then tear the fabric into strips.

- Think about the color combinations of the rug before you start. You could use dye if you have a particular color or effect in mind, or simply go freestyle and opt for the multicolored look.

- Take your first strip and push it into the first grid square and out so that the edge of the canvas square is in the middle of the strip.

- Make a double overhand knot with the fabric strip and pull tight. Then take another strip and push this into the next hole and do the same process until you have your rug!

The great thing about these rag rugs is that they can be washed in the machine as if you were still washing the clothes that they're made of. It's also a craft that doesn't require your undivided attention so you can do it while watching your favorite TV shows.

Be mindful of your water usage

Although there is a plentiful supply of water in the developed world, there are sound reasons for reducing your water usage. By using less water, you will save money and use less energy, not only because you will heat less water but to clean waste water is highly energy-intensive, which impacts the wider world. Here are some practical ways to reduce your water usage.

- Try to limit your showers to 3 to 5 minutes, and by doing so you will save on your energy bills by up to 15 percent.

- Don't keep the tap running when brushing your teeth — this will save around 1 ½ gallons of water per minute.

- Go a step further and simply use a cup of water to dip your brush into and use for mouth-rinsing after brushing.

- Keep your taps in good shape. If they drip, get washers changed — fixing a dripping tap can save up to 15 ¾ gallons of water a week.

- When it comes to boiling a kettle, only boil the amount of water that you need.

- Don't wash your clothes so often!

- Wait until you have a full load of laundry before doing a load — washing a full load uses less energy and water than two half-loads.

- Get a toilet that doesn't require so much water when flushing. Old toilets use around 3 ½ gallons of water per flush, whereas the newer dual-flush systems use around 1 gallon or less. Alternatively, arrange for a cistern displacement device to be installed in your toilet to reduce the volume of water required when flushing — placing a brick in the bottom of your cistern is a quick and effective alternative.

- Invest in an energy-efficient showerhead.

- Use a steamer instead of boiling vegetables — not only does it retain nutrients of vegetables, which is healthier for you, but it uses less water.

- Invest in a rain barrel for your garden to catch rainwater — the most eco-friendly way of watering the garden.

- Use a watering can instead of a hose when watering plants. Hoses use 250 gallons of water per hour. If you do your watering in the early morning and evening, the water will be absorbed more effectively into the ground, as it's less likely to evaporate.

- Invest in a dishwasher — these use up less water than washing by hand, as well as making your items hygienically clean.

- Have a water meter installed — there is no better motivation to save water than when you can see how much you are using and how much it is costing you.

Time to declutter!

The *lagom* home is a calm, tidy space with minimal clutter. It doesn't mean "no"clutter, however; this is where clever storage comes into play. Having a tidy home is important for general happiness and well-being; clear surfaces and a designated place for everything is calming, as you'll get to know where everything is and you won't have the stress of searching for those elusive scissors. The act of tidying can be a calming experience too. It offers a low-impact workout that produces serotonin, the mood-balancing hormone that makes us feel good.

Many of us struggle with having too much stuff, and when it comes to decluttering it's tempting to put it off simply because, well, where do you start? This section will give you a few tips on how to embrace decluttering, and even make it fun!

Clothes

Clothes are a weakness for many of us, but do you really know what you've got, and how much of it do you actually wear? Begin by emptying and sorting one drawer at a time or one closet at a time. For some items you won't need to give much thought to whether to let them go, but others can be tricky. This is when you should ask yourself the following questions:

- Do I love it?

- Do I wear it?

- Does it project the image I want to project?

- Does it itch or scratch?

- Can I actually move in it comfortably?

- When did I last wear it?
  (Will I shrink back into those jeans, like, ever?!)

Be honest, and soon you will have a large pile that can be sorted into categories: to be given away to friends and family, sold on eBay or other sites, shwopped,* or taken to the charity shop.

Here's a great tip to find out which items are not being worn in your wardrobe. Hang your clothes with the hangers all pointing to the right. Then every time you return an item to your wardrobe after wearing it, make sure the hanger is pointing to the left. After a few months you will have a clear picture of what you do and don't wear, which will make your decluttering task that much easier.

*SHWOPPING

This is a trendy word for clothes swapping, and is growing in popularity among the style-savvy and eco-conscious. It's a great example of sustainability, as it means that you can offload the clothes you don't wear or want in exchange for other people's preloved items, rather than heading to the shops to buy more.

Some tips on storing the keepers

Bring a sense of order to your wardrobe by following these simple rules.

- Invest in some good hangers. Your clothes will look less rumpled, so no need to iron.

- Hang items that go together on one hanger, so that you can grab an outfit quickly rather than choosing random garments and spending the day looking as if you got dressed in the dark.*

- Organize your outfits in sections, perhaps by color. Not only does this make it easier to find things, but you'll feel super smug every time you open your closet.

- When you're storing seasonal items, don't forget to weed out anything that you haven't worn recently. Also, remember to dry-clean certain items, such as winter coats, before putting them away.

- This way you can enjoy the clothes you have and make the most of them, as they won't get hidden at the back of the closet.

*A study found that women (and most likely men, too) spend around a year of their lives trying to work out what to wear. Adopting the principle of hanging complete outfits together in the closet will save you time so you can do something more enjoyable!

Clever storage solutions

DIY SHOE STORAGE ▷
HANGERS

First, you will need to hang a rail at the lower part of the closet, leaving enough room between it and the bottom of the closet for your hanger and shoes to fit. Then find some old, wire coat hangers; these will be fashioned into a very nifty unit for stashing shoes. Locate the center point on the bottom wire of the hanger and cut with wire cutters. You are left with two separate lengths that you can bend into shape. Bend one half to

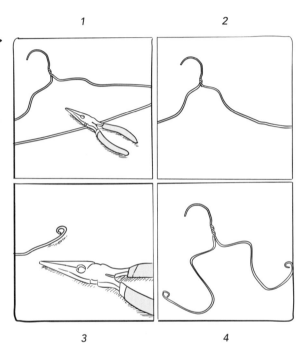

the left and the other to the right, forming two opposing hook shapes. The ends will be sharp so twist them over to make a hoop or spiral, and you have yourself a shoe hanger. Create a hanger for each pair of shoes and hang them up.

VERTICAL CLOTHING ▷

If you store your clothes vertically you will be able to see each item clearly and remove them from the drawer without disrupting the rest of the neatly folded pieces. How easy is that?

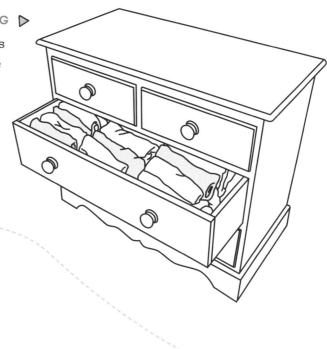

◁ VELCRO TOY STORAGE

Stick a piece of Velcro to the wall. Make sure the rougher side faces outward and then attach fluffy or felted toys. Suspended quite comfortably on the wall, panda, bunny, bear, and mutant caterpillar will actually look tidy... unbelievable.

Branch hooks

If you're looking for extra hanging space but want something a bit different, try these branch hooks for size.

You will need:

One branch per hook

Two screws per hook

Acrylic paint, optional

Paintbrush, if using paint

Saw

Drill

Instructions:

- Take off any excess limbs on your branch and cut the base at a right angle to make it easy to attach to the wall.

- If you want to paint your branches, perhaps to match your décor, then do this now and allow to dry.

- Drill two holes at the base of your branch, then add the screws to the holes and use the drill to drive these into the wall.

- If you have painted your branches, dab some paint over the screws and allow to dry.

- Your hooks are now ready to use.

Try to use windfall branches rather than sawing off tree branches, unless you're coppicing the tree purposefully.

Simplicity is the ultimate sophistication.

LEONARDO DA VINCI

Some tips on decluttering other items in your home

LINEN CLOSET – Unless you run a hotel, you don't need shelves full of spare bed linen. One solution to improve your bed linen storage is to fold duvet covers around matching pillowcases, or, if you're particularly handy at folding, fold the duvet cover and a pillowcase so it fits inside its corresponding pillowcase.

TOY BOX – Allocate storage for each child's toys and encourage them to clean up at night. Extend the life of toys by rotating them every few weeks so that your child plays with their toys until they outgrow them. Children often stop playing with toys because they get bored of them, but having them on rotation (with the ones not in use hidden from sight) encourages them to re-engage with toys that are still age-appropriate.

BOOKS – Go through your books and decide which ones truly deserve a place on your bookshelf and in your life — the ones that moved you, the ones that are too beautiful to part with, the ones that were gifted with inscriptions, the ones autographed by your favorite writer — then be honest about the ones that you are never going to read or refer to again. Take these to a used bookstore, ready to be loved by someone else.

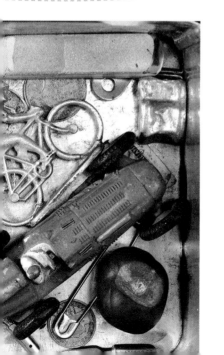

PAPERWORK AND CORRESPONDENCE – It's amazing how quickly receipts fill your purse and statements and household documents multiply into paper monoliths on your desk or kitchen surface. How much of it do you really need? This little guide should help reduce your paper use.

Receipts – Keep receipts for high-ticket items, but discard everyday receipts after a month — many shops and businesses offer to send receipts electronically via e-mail.

Bank statements – Go paperless and check your statements online.

Work/tax documents – Keep paystubs and tax-related documents for two years from the end of the tax year that they relate to. If self-employed, hold onto these documents for six years from the end of the tax year that they relate to.

   With what's left, store in a labeled expanding file folder, and the next time you receive something you want to keep safe, pop it in right away!

Warranties and user guides – Throw away anything pertaining to something that you no longer need or use. Most user guides can be accessed online, but keep the ones for newish products.

Bills – Pay them and then file them, but throw away after a couple of years.

Insurance documents – Keep the valid ones only.

MAGAZINES AND NEWSPAPERS – Cancel subscriptions for magazines that you don't read, and subscribe to online newsagents instead, where you pay a monthly fee for unlimited access to all the latest magazines. Most newspapers offer an online-only subscription too.

   Proudly display the magazines that you are keeping in a rack or in a small(ish) pile on the coffee table, and recycle the ones you don't want or take them to a local doctor's office for their waiting room.

Sustainable shopping – checklist

To reduce clutter, think before you buy. The next time you see something you want to buy, ask yourself the following questions:

- Can I live without it?

- Will I wear it/use it? If so, where and when?

- Can I afford it? Would I prefer to have the money in my account or this item in my house?

- Have I got the space for it?

If you're still not sure, the best thing to do is sleep on it, then go back and buy it the next day if you're convinced you must have it.

> **Tip**
>
> Have a rule that if you buy something you must get rid of something, so you're never adding to your amount of belongings.

Top tips to reduce food waste

Food waste is a big issue — the U.S. alone throws away 60 million tons of produce each year, and the amount of money wasted per household is around $2,200 per year. However, there are some easy fixes to help you reduce food waste in your home, such as:

- Plan your meals for the week and be aware of the amount of food you are purchasing — it might seem tedious, but planning for the week and only buying what you need for all of your meals will avoid waste. Be sure to buy products that won't expire before you plan to cook them.

- Don't be taken in by offers where you end up buying more food than necessary.

- Include big dishes in your menu plan, such as risotto or stew, which can be eaten over a few days, reducing the need to cook every day.

- Store food properly — use airtight containers and keep the fridge tidy so you know what you've got and how long the items will last.

- Make the most of leftovers, e.g. use a roast chicken carcass for stock or a delicious soup (see Lovely leftovers section on page 50 for further ideas).

- Freeze items such as sliced bread for toasting — this will last months, and you will only need to take out the slices you want to eat and pop them in your toaster.

- Eat first before you shop. If you're hungry, you're likely to buy more than you need, and you'll be more inclined to buy sugary snacks.

Tally up all the food and drink items that you throw away over a month. You are likely to see a pattern forming where the same items are ending up in the trash, such as salads, bread, meals that you buy in offers that seem good value but you don't really want to eat, certain fruit that has become overripe, the same things that get discarded in lunchboxes. If you don't like something, don't buy it in the first place! But similarly, some items don't need to be thrown away when they're slightly past their prime.

The difference between "best before" and "use by" dates

The "best before" date refers to the optimum quality of a product and it is still safe to eat beyond this date. It's important, however, that the food item is stored as specified on the label. The "use by" date refers to safety, and food should be discarded after this date.

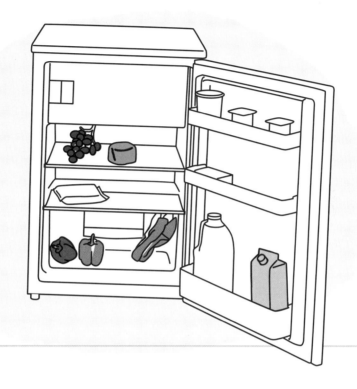

FOOD SHOPPING HACK

How often have you gone food shopping and not been able to remember whether you have or haven't got something only to buy it and get home to find you do already have it? How frustrating! With this simple hack, you will never encounter this irritation again.

Take a photo of the contents of your fridge and cabinets before leaving to do your weekly shopping trip. By doing this, you can look at the images and see what you do and don't need.

Extending the life of food

We're spoiled when it comes to food selection and expect to only eat items when they're at their best and ripest, but some items don't need to be ditched if they're past their prime. Fruit that's gone a bit soft might not seem appealing to eat but can make the ideal ingredient for smoothies, jams, and chutneys. Here are some tips on what to do with an abundance of fruit or vegetables:

- Strawberries, raspberries, blueberries, and wild fruits can be frozen. Open-freeze the fruits by spreading them on trays and placing directly in the freezer. Once frozen, transfer them into plastic bags and seal them. This stops them from sticking to each other.

- All fruits can be dried, but only use blemish-free fruits for this. Wash, pit, and slice the fruits, then blanch them by steaming for five minutes then plunging the pieces into cold water. Dip them in a mixture of water and lemon juice to reduce browning and leave them to dry on a kitchen towel. Once completely dry, place on parchment-lined baking trays and place them in the oven on low heat for 4 hours. Let them stand overnight and then freeze them in sealed bags until required.

- Pears and apples should be wrapped individually in newspaper and stored in wooden boxes or drawers in a cool, dark place. An unheated garage or shed is ideal. Check on the fruits regularly for ones that have gone bad.

- If you have the shed or garage space, pick up an old chest of drawers from a junk shop and use it to store your root vegetables. Spread a layer of sand at the bottom of each drawer and place a layer of vegetables on top. Then cover the vegetables with sand and add more vegetables on top until you reach the top of the drawer. Label and date the drawers.

- Potatoes can be scrubbed and stored in burlap sacks in a cool, dry place.

- Don't discard windfall fruit; it can be used to make delicious chutney, or frozen and later defrosted to provide a treat for birds in the depths of winter.

Caramelized Onion Chutney

This is heavenly with a cheese board and crackers!

MAKES 4 (8-OUNCE) JARS

Ingredients:

7 large red onions

1 large white onion

2 shallots

Olive oil

A sprig of fresh rosemary

2 bay leaves (fresh is best)

1 red chile

1 sweet red pepper
  (piquillo is good)

1 cup balsamic vinegar

¼ cup red wine vinegar

1 cup dark brown sugar

4 (8-ounce) sterilized jam jars*

Method:

- Peel and chop the onions and shallots into ½-inch cubes.

- Add a dash of olive oil into a pan over low heat and fry the onions and shallots for 10 minutes until soft and golden.

- Remove the rosemary leaves from the branch and chop, then add to the onions along with the bay leaves.

- Seed and dice the chile and sweet pepper and stir into the mixture. Allow to cook for a few minutes.

- Stir in the balsamic and red wine vinegar and dark brown sugar and simmer until it begins to thicken and starts to resemble chutney.

- Spoon into your prepared jam jars and screw on the lids. The chutney will keep for up to six weeks stored in a cool, dry place. Refrigerate once opened.

* The simplest way to sterilize jars is to heat in an oven at 275°F. Wash the jars in hot, soapy water, then rinse well. Place the jars, still wet, on a baking sheet and put them in the oven to dry completely.

Strawberry Jam

Of all the summer fruits, strawberries seem to be the most ubiquitous. Here's a fail-safe recipe for the perfect accompaniment to morning toast.

MAKES 2 (4-OUNCE) JARS

Ingredients:

1 ¼ pounds strawberries

1 ¼ cups sugar

1 ½ tablespoons fresh lemon
 juice

Sterilized jam jars

Method:

- Place the strawberries in a large saucepan, bring slowly to boiling point, and then simmer for 5 minutes.

- Add in the sugar, stir, and leave to simmer for 10–15 minutes. Remove the pan from the heat and stir in the lemon juice.

- Pour the jam into sterilized jars (see page 47) and seal with a lid. Leave to set and cool. The jam will keep for at least a year if stored in a cool, dry cupboard, but once opened it must be stored in a fridge.

Lovely leftovers

Do you often cook enough for a family of six when there are only two of you? Good, I'm glad it's not just me, but what do you do with the leftovers? Throw them in the trash, or perhaps put them in some Tupperware and leave it to languish at the back of the fridge until mold starts to form? Well, it's time to stop. We all know that throwing food away is the equivalent of throwing your money in the trash. It's time to get creative with your leftovers. Here are some ways to make them last longer. This is the fun part of saving food waste!

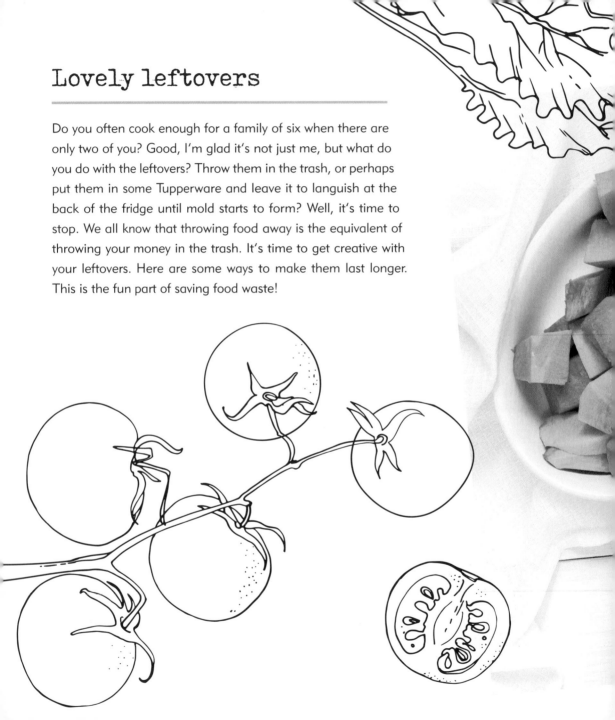

Twice-Baked Potatoes

This recipe works well if you've cooked too many hot potatoes! Just multiply the basic recipe to make more servings.

MAKES 1 SERVING

Ingredients:

1 baking potato per person

Olive oil

Salt

3 ½ ounces button mushrooms, sliced

1 red pepper, deseeded and cut into small chunks

Bacon, chopped
(1 strip per person)

1 (8-ounce) tub sour cream

Good pinch dried mixed herbs

Grated cheese

To serve (optional):

A dollop of sour cream

A handful of chopped green onions

Method:

- Preheat your oven to 350°F.

- Pierce your potatoes and then rub them with olive oil and salt until coated.

- Place in the oven to cook for 1 hour 15 minutes or until soft. Meanwhile, fry the mushrooms, pepper, and bacon in a small pan over medium heat for 5 to 7 minutes. Set aside.

- Slice each potato in half and scoop out the insides. Place the empty skins back in the oven to crisp for a few minutes.

- Place the potato insides into a bowl with the mushrooms, pepper, and bacon.

- Mix several dollops of sour cream into the bowl with the potatoes, mushrooms, mixed herbs, pepper, and bacon until the mixture looks clumpy. Spoon back inside the potato cases and cook for 10 minutes more.

- Sprinkle with cheese and bake for another 5 minutes.

- Top with a spoonful of sour cream and chopped green onions. Serve immediately.

Tikki Aloo

This is a traditional snack served in north India, Bangladesh, and Pakistan. It's often served with chutney for dipping.

MAKES 12 PATTIES

Ingredients:

Leftover baked potatoes

2 handfuls frozen peas, boiled

4 tablespoons cornmeal

4 tablespoons breadcrumbs,
   plus more to coat

1 teaspoon red chili powder

1 teaspoon garam masala

1 teaspoon freshly grated
   ginger

1 teaspoon fresh lemon juice

3 teaspoons oil

To serve (optional):

Fresh coriander leaves

Method:

- Remove the soft potato flesh from the skins and mash until all lumps are removed.

- Add the peas, 4 tablespoons of the breadcrumbs, cornmeal, chili powder, garam masala, ginger, and lemon juice and stir until combined.

- Roll into small balls and then press into patties. Pour extra breadcrumbs onto a plate and press the patties into them to coat each side.

- Heat the oil in a nonstick frying pan and fry the patties for 3 to 4 minutes on each side until golden brown and cooked through.

- You can freeze after coating with breadcrumbs to store for later.

- Serve with fresh coriander leaves sprinkled on top.

Tip

If you're heating up leftovers instead of creating something new, using the microwave will use less energy than turning on the oven.

Sausage Roast

This hearty recipe is wonderful on a cold day. It's also a great way to use up stray vegetables and that pack of sausages that's been sitting in the freezer.

SERVES 4

Ingredients:

1 tablespoon olive oil

2 ¼ pounds sweet potatoes, peeled and cut into wedges

3 large mixed-colored peppers, deseeded and cut into chunks

1 pound sausages (about 6)

1 tablespoon mixed herbs

2 large red onions, peeled and quartered

4 garlic cloves, peeled

To serve (optional):

A sprinkling of fresh parsley

Method:

- Preheat the oven to 350°F.

- Pour the olive oil into a deep roasting pan and heat for 5 minutes in the oven.

- Add the sweet potatoes, peppers, and sausages to the roasting pan and toss thoroughly in the oil. Add the herbs and roast for another 20 minutes.

- Spread the onion quarters and the garlic about the pan and return to the oven for another 15 minutes.

- Remove, toss in the oil, and cook for another 10 minutes, ensuring the potatoes are cooked and the sausages are browned.

- Add a sprinkle of parsley and serve with steamed green vegetables such as cabbage, leeks, or broccoli.

Leftover Roasted Vegetable Tart

This delicious tart can be made from leftover vegetables from the sausage roast, or any roast for that matter.

SERVES 4

Ingredients:

Butter, for greasing

1 (9-inch) prepared pie dough

1 egg, beaten

4 to 6 cups leftover vegetables

A few sprigs fresh thyme, parsley, or chives

Goat cheese

Method:

- Preheat the oven to 350°F.

- Grease a 9-inch pie dish with the butter.

- Unroll the dough and place over the pie dish. Gently push the dough into the base and sides. Trim the excess pastry from the edges, leaving an overhang of 1 inch. Pinch the edges to finish it off.

- Prick the base of the dough with a fork and wash the border with the beaten egg. Bake blind using pie weights for approximately 5 minutes.

- Arrange the vegetables in the baked crust and dot with thyme and goat cheese.

- Bake for 15 minutes more or until the pastry is golden.

- Serve hot with salad or chips.

Tip

If you're short on time but want to have a hot, nutritious meal when you get home in the evening, invest in a slow cooker. This is one-step, one-pot cooking and it couldn't be simpler. They also use less electricity than a conventional oven and with the longer low-temperature cooking time, they help to tenderize cheaper cuts of meat, as well as bringing out the flavors in food. Many meals can be created in a slow-cooker, such as stews, casseroles, and soups.

Eat seasonal, eat local

Living *lagom* also means reducing our impact on the environment, so think about eating seasonally, buying locally sourced foods, or even growing your own. Lists of seasonal vegetables for grocery shopping are available online, as they vary depending on the country you live in.

To give you an idea of the carbon footprint* of some foods, a study found that meat and dairy products produce the highest amount of carbon emissions due to the preparation methods and animal husbandry required. For example, producing and eating 2¼ pounds of beef produces the same amount of carbon dioxide as driving 60 miles in an average-sized car.

* A carbon footprint is the amount of carbon dioxide emitted into the atmosphere as the direct result of the activities of an individual, organization, or community. Go to nature.org/greenliving/carboncalculator to discover your impact on the environment in terms of the products that you buy, your energy consumption, ways that you travel, and technology you use.

The Lagom Garden

If you're looking to eat food that is locally sourced, you can't get any more local, or convenient, than your own garden or windowsill. This is a wonderful way to further reduce your carbon footprint and encourage healthy eating in your family. The physical benefits of gardening are also worth considering: Working in the garden can be as challenging as any aerobics class, and the exertion releases endorphins, which alleviate stress and lower blood pressure.

If you live in an apartment with no outside space, that doesn't have to stop you. A window box or pots on a windowsill can be enough to grow a range of fresh fruit, vegetables, and herbs, saving you quite a few dollars on your grocery bill, especially if you're always buying bags of salad and herbs. Community gardening initiatives are another way to develop your green thumb and grow your own produce.

Salad leaves and herbs can be grown in the kitchen (away from direct sunlight), ensuring fresh leaves all year round. Think of how much you spend on salad throughout the year, maybe $2.50 per week — that's a saving of over $125! Home-grown tastes best, too, and reduces your carbon footprint in terms of consumables.

Get growing

Empty toilet paper rolls make ideal containers for growing crops from seeds, especially loose-leaf lettuce — Tom Thumb and Baby Oakleaf are good varieties to grow indoors. Fold in one end of the toilet roll to create a spill-proof container. Fill the container halfway with compost and moisten with water, then add a little starting mix before placing a seed in each container. Add a covering of potting soil to cover the seeds and then moisten with water. It's advisable to place your toilet roll planters on a waterproof tray so that the water doesn't soak through onto your windowsill or floor. A sunny spot will help the seedlings to sprout, such as a greenhouse or windowsill — you can grow lettuce year-round this way. Keep an eye on the moisture level of your plants and within as little as four weeks you will have your first crop of lettuce! Trim the outer leaves with kitchen scissors, and it's ready to eat. If you have space in a garden, you can plant the whole plant — including the container — into the ground (or in larger pots outdoors). The cardboard will protect the roots from pests before it biodegrades.

Grow your own herbs in jam jars

These are not only decorative but they're a neat way of growing your own herbs on your kitchen windowsill.

You will need:

A selection of jam jars

Small stones

Potting compost

Young herb plants, such as parsley, thyme, basil, oregano, coriander, rosemary, mint, or chive (you can purchase these from supermarkets or garden centers)

Water

Instructions:

● Clean your jam jars with dishwashing soap and warm water, then rinse and leave to dry.

● Fill the base of your jars with stones — make sure it's a minimum of 2 inches deep. These stones are vital, as they will draw the water up and prevent mold from forming on your plants.

● Fill the jars about two-thirds full with potting soil.

● Remove the baby herb plants from their containers and gently tap the roots with your fingers to loosen the soil around it. Then plant the baby herbs in the jars — one per jar.

● Add more potting soil to the top and pat it down around the base of the each plant.

● Then water your plants, and they're ready to be placed on a windowsill. Make sure they are not in direct sunlight.

Now you can enjoy herbs year-round, and they're easy to grab when you're preparing meals.

Drying herbs for year-round use

Sturdy herbs, such as dill, bay, rosemary, and oregano, can be air-dried on a windowsill. Moisture-rich herbs, such as basil, lemon balm, and mint, are best oven-dried so that they dry out more quickly to avoid mold.

Before air-drying herbs, cut and remove any dry or diseased leaves. Shake gently to remove any insects or rinse with cool water and pat dry with paper towels (wet herbs will mold and rot). Remove the lower leaves along the bottom inch or so of each branch. Bundle four to six branches together and tie as a bunch using string or a rubber band, then leave these on a windowsill or a sunny spot in the house. You can even hang them up by making a makeshift clothes line and using clothespins to keep them in place. The bundles will shrink as they dry and the rubber band will loosen, so check periodically that the bundles are not slipping.

For sturdier herbs such as rosemary, make small bundles for drying, tying the bunches together with string or a rubber band as before. Punch or cut several holes in a paper bag. Label the bag with the name of the herb to be dried and place the herb bundle upside down in the bag. Gather the ends of the bag around the bundle and tie closed. Make sure the herbs are not crowded inside the bag. Hang the bag upside down in a warm, airy room and check in about two weeks to see how things are progressing. Keep checking weekly until the herbs are dry and ready to store.

Once dried, store your herbs in airtight containers in a cool, dark place. They should remain fresh for up to two years.

Compost it!

If food items aren't salvagable, try composting. You can make your own compost if you have a garden or community plot. Many items can be composted to produce nutrient-rich soil to grow plants.

HOW TO START COMPOSTING

- Purchase a bin or designate an area of the garden for a pile, which must be a minimum of one cubic yard. If you're making a pile, be aware that the items that you place on the pile may attract wildlife, so make sure it is a good distance from your house and away from where children might want to play. It also needs to be in an area with good drainage and in a part-sunny/part-shaded spot.

- Prepare a layer of twigs and branches at the bottom of the pile to provide vertical airflow through the material; on top of this mix in your browns and greens* with thin layers of dead flowers, manure, and straw. Sheep manure is probably the richest source of nutrients, just ahead of horse manure. Chances are you can probably find both for free if you know a farmer or horse owner.

- Don't add the following items to your compost pile: charcoal or coal ashes, which contain high amounts of sulphur; cat or dog droppings, which might contain disease; or weeds, which will only return disease back to the soil once you spread your compost. And unless you want to attract rats to your garden, avoid adding eggs or meat to the mix.

- Weed-free and pesticide-free grass clippings bring nitrogen to your compost — so be sure to mix them in well with the browns to avoid smells, prevent a slimy texture, and get the maximum benefit from the grass. Let the worms get to work!

- If you want your compost pile to remain active during winter, be sure to keep your bin in a place that gets lots of sunlight so that the compost can form quickly. Alternatively, insulate the sides with hay to keep the compost warm.

- Turn your compost pile every two weeks for fast results. The finished compost should look and smell like rich, dark soil and have a crumbly rather than sticky texture. Compost can be made in six to eight weeks, or it can take a year or more. The more effort you put in, the quicker you get results.

- Your compost pile should be moist all the way through, so be sure to wet each new layer every time you add one. Do not leave a finished compost pile standing unprotected, as it will lose nutrients. Special breathable compost cover sheets can be found at any garden center.

* Browns and greens refer to the different items that you can compost. Green items are fresh, moist items (not necessarily green!), such as grass clippings and vegetable peelings, whereas brown items are dry, older items, such as dead leaves, wood shavings, and pieces of cardboard. The green items are nitrogen-rich, whereas the brown items are carbon-rich, and the most successful compost piles contain a balance of the two.

Make a bug hotel

Attract solitary bees and other insects to the garden with this simple bug hotel. This is a great way to repurpose items that you're likely to have on hand.

You will need:

Scissors

An empty plastic 2-liter bottle

String

Bamboo poles (these must be hollow but can be of varying sizes)

Instructions:

- Use your scissors to carefully cut off the top and bottom of the bottle, leaving the center tube. Place the base and the top of the bottle in the recycling.

- Make two small holes (big enough to thread string through) about halfway down the bottle, and about 2 inches apart.

- Push one end of the string into each of the holes and pull a small section through. Then knot each end and pull out the string so you have a way to hang up your bug hotel.

- Take a piece of bamboo and cut it in equal lengths that are a few inches longer than the bottle. Take another piece of bamboo and do the same again until you have enough poles so that when they are slotted into the bottle they are packed together tightly and don't move.

- When it is finished, hang up your bug hotel so the bottle is on its side and the bamboo lies horizontally in the bottle. Be careful to pick a spot that gets some sunshine in the day but is sheltered from wind.

Amazingly cheap and simple upcycling ideas for the garden

- Make a garden kneeler by filling an old hot-water bottle with packing peanuts. It's wipe-clean and will make those long hours in the garden a little more comfortable.

- An ice-cream container can be cut up to make multiple waterproof plant markers.

- Curtain rods, particularly extendable ones, are perfect for training tall climbing plants. Simply extend the rod as the plant grows!

- Don't spend money on support poles; use twigs instead. They look far less conspicuous and they're free!

- Save packaging from store-bought food items — trays and cartons can be used to plant seedlings. Supermarkets regularly throw out wooden and plastic crates which make great planters.

- When you've finished with plastic drink bottles, make cloches by cutting the bottoms off. Place firmly in the ground to protect the plants from slugs, and remove the bottle tops when the plants are more established to allow them to acclimatize.

- The next time you have a cup of tea, don't throw the tea bag away. Instead, tear it open and sprinkle the dregs on the lawn as an instant fertilizer. Coffee grounds are equally beneficial.

mint

- Using old spare tires as planters for potatoes or carrots is eco-friendly and effective. For carrots, a sandy-mix soil in a two-tire-deep container will give you lovely, straight crops, free of pests (carrot flies can only fly to around 2 feet so if the tire wall is high enough they cannot attack young plants). For potatoes, plant sprouted tubers one tire deep, wait for shoots to grow, bank up with soil, and add more tires to the stack (up to about three tires deep). Once the plants have flowered the potatoes are ready to harvest.

- Ash from a bonfire, once cooled, is rich potash for fruit trees. Spread the ash around the base of fruit trees for a bumper harvest.

- Cuttings are one of the best ways to propagate new plants in your garden for free. If a neighbor or friend has a plant that you like the look of, take a cutting — but make sure you ask first!

- Another way to obtain free seeds and seedlings is to join the Seed Savers Exchange initiative. Through this site, people can offload their excess seedlings. Visit seedsavers.org to find out more.

PART 2

A Balanced Diet and Good Health

It's important to remember that although there is an element of frugality in *lagom*, it isn't about abstinence but achieving a healthy balance that works for you — remember, "not too much, not too little, just the right amount." In terms of diet and good health, this constitutes eating a varied diet combined with regular exercise and not denying yourself the odd treat now and then.

Mood-balancing foods

There are foods that are said to be good for the heart, the brain, and digestion — and there are foods that increase or reduce stress levels. A balanced diet means eating the right amount of calories for your age, height, and sex, and ensuring you get enough protein, fiber, and vitamin-rich fruits and vegetables to give you a sound basis for general health and good digestion. Eating a balanced diet puts you in the best shape to fight stress and illness, and acts as an excellent starting point for long-term health.

STABILIZE YOUR BLOOD SUGAR

When we keep our blood sugar stable we provide our body with the steady supply of energy; our hormones are in check, we feel happy, we get glowing skin and an even skin tone, and we begin to shed the extra pounds naturally and effortlessly. If your blood sugar levels are racing up and down like a roller coaster, you'll inevitably feel less well and, over time, serious health concerns can result. By making simple but specific adjustments to your lifestyle and diet, you can gain better blood-sugar control.

DON'T SKIP MEALS

It's important to spread out your daily food intake, starting with breakfast. Consuming more food in just one or two meals a day causes greater fluctuations in blood sugar levels. Instead, aim to eat three healthy meals a day with two nutritious snacks, such as a handful of nuts or carrot sticks dipped in hummus, to help maintain stable blood sugar.

KEEP YOUR GI LOW

GI stands for glycemic index. This is a measurement of how much energy a food will give you from sugars. High-GI foods tend to be things like sweets and pastries, while vegetables and lean protein such as fish, skinless chicken, and tofu are low GI.

A low-GI diet can have many health benefits, including aiding weight loss, and is particularly good for combating stress. High-GI foods will cause a spike in blood sugar, which will then drop rapidly, leaving you feeling tired, irritable, and hungry again. This is the perfect formula for feeling stressed. Low-GI foods, on the other hand, help keep blood sugar levels more steady, avoiding those dips and helping you feel calmer.

ENOUGH GOOD FATS

Although we are often told that eating a low-fat diet is healthy, certain fats are needed for optimum health. In fact, certain fats help ensure your brain and immune system function properly. Making sure you include some of these good fats in your diet can help to reduce the negative effects of stress on your body, and help your body to cope better with stress.

The four main types of fat are monounsaturated, polyunsaturated, saturated, and trans. It is the first two types that you need in your diet, and these can be found in foods such as fish, nuts, seeds, olive oil, and avocados.

BE ACE

Aim to eat plenty of foods rich in the antioxidant vitamins A, C, and E. These antioxidants help normalize the body and reduce inflammation while boosting immunity.

Vitamin A is found in the form of retinol in products such as fish liver oil and egg yolks. Too much retinol can be bad for the health though, so balance this with beta-carotene, found in mainly yellow and orange fruits and vegetables, such as carrots, butternut squash, and apricots. Vitamin C is found in good amounts in citrus fruits, broccoli, berries, and tomatoes, and vitamin E is found in nuts, seeds, avocados, olive oil, and wheat germ. Adding some of these foods to your diet could make you feel healthier and happier.

LESS SALT

Being stressed can make us crave salt, as our adrenal glands become exhausted and are unable to make adrenaline and cortisol. This results in a salt imbalance and it can be very easy to reach for salty foods — especially as many of these foods are also fatty and comforting. Although high salt intake alone does not increase stress levels, the associated health problems such as weight gain and high blood pressure certainly do, so give the salt a wide berth. Instead, choose fruit as a snack and prepare your meals from fresh produce, as pre-packaged foods are usually very high in salt.

GET A B-VIT BOOST

The B vitamin group is particularly important for maintaining a healthy balance and keeping stress at bay. Among their other functions, B vitamins are involved in the body's control of tryptophan, a building block for serotonin. Too little tryptophan can lead to a drop of serotonin which can lead to low mood. The main vitamins to pay attention to are B1, B2, B3, B5, B6, B7, B9, and B12, all of which can be found in a balanced diet, especially in foods such as spinach, broccoli, asparagus, and liver. If you eat a lot of processed foods, or are a vegan, you may be lacking in certain B vitamins, in which case adding a B-vitamin supplement to your diet can have an excellent effect.

Moderate your stimulants

CAFFEINE

Caffeine and other similar stimulants should be avoided as much as possible. Many of us rely on that first cup of coffee in the morning to wake us up, or a cup of tea to keep us going at midday, but these caffeinated drinks, along with cola and foods containing caffeine, such as chocolate, could be having an adverse effect on your stress levels — perhaps the opposite effect to the one you intend.

Drinking a caffeinated drink can make us feel more alert because it induces the initial stages of the stress reaction, boosting cortisol production. Consuming large quantities of caffeine, however, can cause the exhaustion phase of stress. Added to this, caffeine can be very addictive, and stopping suddenly can cause withdrawal symptoms. Try cutting down slowly to no more than 300 mg of caffeine in a day — that's the equivalent of three mugs of coffee or four mugs of tea in a day. Have fun experimenting with the huge variety of herbal teas available on the market to fill the gap or try a non-caffeinated version.

ALCOHOL

After a hard day at work, many people will reach for a drink to help them relax. Alcohol does have a calming effect, but this is negated by the depressant qualities of alcohol and the feeling of anxiety that can be left behind once the effects wear off. Alcohol can also disturb sleep, contrary to the popular idea of a "nightcap." Try to cut down drinking as much as possible, and, if you do go for a sip, opt for a small glass of Chianti, Merlot, or Cabernet Sauvignon, as the grape skins used in these wines are rich with the sleep hormone, melatonin. All good things in moderation, though!

Red Currant Smoothie

Smoothies are a great way of using up excess soft fruits. Be creative and experiment with different flavor combinations such as blueberries or raspberries.

SERVES 2

Ingredients:

8 ounces red currants,
   fresh or frozen

1 small banana, peeled

5 tablespoons black currant
   and apple cordial

1 cup natural yogurt

Red currants and fresh mint
   leaves to garnish

Method:

- Remove any stalks from the red currants.

- Place the red currants, banana, cordial, and yogurt in a blender and blend on high speed for a minute or two.

- If you are using frozen red currants the smoothie will be a good temperature, but if you are using fresh red currants you may want to chill before consuming.

- Sprinkle a few red currants and mint leaves on top of the smoothie to serve.

Swedish Open Sandwich with Gravlax

Gravlax is a popular Nordic dish and is often served as an appetizer, but this recipe makes for a delicious snack.

SERVES 4

Ingredients:

Approx. 2 pounds salmon fillets

1 medium-sized bunch dill, roughly chopped

4 tablespoons coarse sea salt

3 ½ tablespoons sugar

2 tablespoons crushed peppercorns

Bread of your choice

To serve (optional):

Red onion slices

Hard-boiled eggs

Lime wedges or slices

Cream cheese

Method:

- Arrange half of the salmon, skin-side down, on a large sheet of plastic wrap. Mix the dill with the salt, sugar, and crushed peppercorns and spread it over the salmon. Place the remainder of the salmon on top, skin-side up.

- Tightly wrap in 2 or 3 layers of plastic wrap and place in a shallow tray. Then place a chopping board on top of the fish to weigh it down. Refrigerate for 2 days. A brine-like liquid will form inside the plastic wrap pouch — use this to baste the fish by turning the fillets every 12 hours.

- Remove the plastic wrap and drain the excess fluid, then finely slice the fish so it's ready to serve with your sandwich. It's a perfect match when paired with red onion slices, hard-boiled eggs, and a squeeze of lime juice served on rye bread with cream cheese.

Portion size guide

Regardless of eating a healthy diet, eating too much or too little can be bad for you — aim for "just the right amount." Here is the suggested portion intake for an average adult in order to receive the necessary daily nutritional requirements:

Starch — 6–8 portions per day
The following count as one portion each: ¾ ounce of breakfast cereal, a slice of bread or toast, two small white potatoes, or 2 ¾ ounces of pasta or rice.

Protein — 2 portions per day
The following count as one portion each: two eggs, a small can of baked beans or chickpeas, a handful of nuts, 2½ ounces of turkey or chicken, 5 ounces of fish, two sausages.

Calcium – 2 portions per day
The following count as one portion each: a container of yogurt or cottage cheese (or nondairy equivalent), a glass of milk (dairy or nondairy), ¾ ounce of hard cheese, a handful of dried fruit.

Fruit and vegetables – at least 5 portions per day
The following count as one portion each: a medium-sized fruit or vegetable, a handful of beans, dried fruit, a fruit or vegetable smoothie (approx. ½ cup).

Fats – limit these if you can to one portion per day, and aim to reduce to every other day.

EAT CAKE, BUT DON'T EAT THE WHOLE CAKE (ADMITTEDLY, THIS IS A TOUGH ONE)

The next time you seek out a sugary snack, stop and think about how you are feeling. People often turn to food in an attempt to self-soothe or deal with stressful situations. Recognize that you are looking for something to eat that you think will bring you satisfaction. Sit down and be fully present with this craving. Awareness can often lessen the desire. Maybe you don't need that chocolate cookie after all!

Hydrate yourself

Dehydration won't disturb your calmness on its own, but if you are already suffering from stress and tension, it may aggravate your condition. If you are prone to panic attacks, it's especially important to stay hydrated as this will lessen the chances of you experiencing common symptoms, which could trigger an attack, such as headaches, feeling light-headed, muscle weakness, and an increased heart rate. The USDA recommends 91 ounces of water a day for women and 125 ounces for men, so try to get used to carrying a bottle of water around with you, and take frequent drinks to stay hydrated. Don't forget that hot drinks, fruit juices, and food also contain water, and so count toward your recommended daily intake.

Be in love with your life,
every detail of it.

JACK KEROUAC

Find the exercise that's right for you

Have you ever noticed how good you feel after a swim, a brisk walk, or a jog? It's the release of the "happy" chemicals endorphins and dopamine, and the reduction in the stress hormones cortisol and adrenalin that makes you feel so good. According to research, just 20 minutes of exercise can boost your mood for up to 12 hours. The following tips will help you get moving and start to feel the mood-boosting benefits of regular exercise.

TAKE A WALK

Walking is such a simple form of exercise, and can be incorporated into your daily life with ease. Though not as fat-busting as running or martial arts, for example, adding regular walking into your routine will help keep you fitter and healthier, and will help reduce feelings of anxiety as it will help your body produce serotonin.

Even if you lead a very busy life, walking can fit in to your routine. Try parking farther from the office, taking the stairs rather than the elevator, or going for a brisk fifteen-minute walk at lunchtime. It is a healthy habit to form and you will soon be reaping the benefits.

SWIM

Swimming is one of the best forms of exercise, both in terms of giving you a full-body work-out which leaves you tired for the right reasons, and in allowing you to relax and unwind. The rhythmic lap of the water with each stroke, and the focus on your technique and breathing, really make this a great way to move your mind away from the stresses of your day. Add to that the fact that floating in water is a wonderfully calming experience — and the best part of a trip to the pool — and you've got a perfect recipe for relaxation.

YOGA

Yoga is an ancient form of exercise that originates from India. It has become very popular in recent years, and with good reason. As well as being a calming form of exercise, it can also be very beneficial in releasing stress from the body. Yoga combines movements with breathing, so that the mind is focused on what the body is doing. This physical focus helps the mind to relax and stop thinking about the worries of the day. Why not try a class near you, or look for tutorials online?

Yoga poses to incorporate into your daily life:

Whenever you find yourself standing still, practice **Mountain**. Inhale: Engage your legs and thighs, stabilize your core, lift through your chest. Exhale: Roll your shoulders back and pull them down the spine.

Be still in **Standing Half Forward Bend** to strengthen your back while stimulating your internal organs. From a Standing Full Forward Bend, inhale and lift your torso parallel to the earth, rest your palms on your shins, or your thighs. Hold. Release the position as you exhale.

 Strengthen your arms and shoulders in **Plank**. Lie on your front, ensuring your wrists are below your shoulders and your feet are either hip-distance apart or big toes and heels touching. Maintain a straight line between your back and your legs and lift your body off the mat. Hold and breathe in position. Build your stamina by holding the pose a little longer each day.

Give a powerful stretch to the whole body in **Downward Dog**. Start in Plank. Inhale. As you exhale, lift your tailbone skyward, push back with your hands, and bring your heels toward the earth.

Breathe in **Lunge** to encourage muscle relief in your groin and thighs. Start on all fours, with your wrists under your shoulders, knees under your hips, and wrists in line with your ankles. Inhale: Bring your left foot between your hands, with toes and fingertips in line. Exhale: Look forward and up to keep the shoulders from rounding forward and let your hips sink a little lower, without crashing all your weight into your lower back. Repeat on the other side.

Feel steady and strong in **Warrior I**. Start in Lunge. Inhale: Straighten and extend your right leg back, keep your opposite knee bent and stacked directly over your ankle. Exhale: Squeeze into your stomach to stabilize your lower back. Inhale: Bring your hands above your head. Repeat, stretching out your left leg.

Connect with your inner spirit in **Warrior II**. Start in Mountain. Inhale: Step back with your left foot. Exhale: Bend your right knee and stack it directly over your ankle. Inhale. Exhale: Extend your right arm forward, your left arm behind. Keep your torso lifted and arms straight. Hold for as long as you feel strong. Repeat on the other side.

Sit in **Staff** to lengthen your hamstrings and to improve your posture. Sit with both legs extended. Inhale: Use your hands to pull the flesh of your buttocks away from your tailbone to connect your "sit bones" to your mat. Exhale: Lengthen your spine and place your palms to the earth.

Invigorate your energy flow in **Seated Forward Bend**. Begin in Staff. Inhale: Raise your hands above your head. Exhale: Hinge from the hips and fold forward, keeping your spine straight. Hold your shins, ankles, or toes depending on your flexibility and breathe for as long as you feel comfortable.

Gently flex your spine in **Cow**. Start on all fours, with your wrists under your shoulders, knees under your hips, and wrists in line with your ankles. Inhale: Tip your tailbone skyward, dip your navel toward the floor, lift your head. Exhale: Tilt your head back, look skyward.

To increase the energy flow in your spine, practice **Cat**. Start on all fours. Inhale. Exhale: Curl your tailbone, arch your back, and look toward your navel. Breathe. Hold and then release.

Release emotional energy stored in your hips by practicing **Bridge**. Lie on your back. Inhale. Exhale: Bend your knees and place your feet on the floor, with your hands down at your hips, arms flat against the floor. Inhale: Push your hips into the air and stabilize yourself using your arms. Hold and breathe for as long as you feel comfortable.

Just breathe

A simple way to start training your body to relax is to practice mindful deep breathing. This can be done at any time of the day, whether before bed, first thing in the morning, or at your desk in the office. The practice is simple: Close your eyes and focus on your breath. Think only about your breath and the way it feels coming into your body and then out. Once you are fully aware of your breathing, try taking deeper breaths, breathing in for a count of six and then out for a count of six. Stay focused on your breath for five minutes. Integrating this exercise into your daily routine will help you on the way to feeling more relaxed.

A balanced mind

Stress is a common occurrence for many of us and affects people in a variety of different ways. The right amount of pressure pushes us to achieve our goals and meet deadlines, but if left unchecked, stress can have a very negative effect. An excess of stress can leave us feeling tired, irritable, and even very unwell. As individuals, we all have different needs. This also means that we have different stress factors in our lives. Although we tend to just live with it, there are some simple ways to reduce stress by identifying and controlling the causes. While there are several broad factors, which would cause stress in anybody, we know ourselves best, and can work out which areas affect us the most. It may be that driving to work makes you stressed, or calling your bank. If so, why not try cycling to work, or talking to someone in person at the local branch of your bank? Identifying these simple triggers and making small changes is the first step to de-stressing your life.

Over the course of two weeks, write down all the things that make you feel stressed, be they places, people, or situations. Rate these stresses on a scale from one to ten, with one being only slightly stressful, and ten being the most stressful. Once you have identified your high-stress triggers you can take steps to eliminate them.

POSITIVE VS. NEGATIVE THINKING

We will all experience difficult situations at some point in our lives, but it is how we deal with them, and not the situations themselves, that has the most impact on our stress levels. A great way to change your mind about problems is to find a positive within the negative.

This can be hard at first, especially in situations that can have quite a strong and lasting effect on your life. Even finding a small positive will make a situation easier to deal with. Perhaps you have lost your job, but the positive is that now you can retrain for the career you always wanted. Or perhaps a relationship has ended, but the positive is that you are now free to find someone more suited to you and form a brighter future. It is not always easy to do this, but this shift in perspective can be very liberating.

SLOW DOWN!

The first thing to do to help build a healthier attitude toward yourself is to simply slow down. Many of us are living our lives at an ever-faster pace, and trying to balance a whole range of commitments from work to family to relationships. This can leave us feeling stressed and frustrated when we are forced to stop, for instance when we have to wait in line. Combat this by taking those moments when your bus is late, or when you are stuck in traffic, to do something relaxing like deep breathing or listening to music.

HAVE A GIGGLE

The old adage tells us that "laughter is the best medicine." In many ways, this is true. Laughter helps us feel relaxed — it relieves tension and makes us feel happier, which in turn leaves us better equipped to deal with the difficult situations life might throw our way.

Try watching your favorite comedy or looking at a funny website for a bit of light relief. You could even invite some friends over for a night of funny movies and to swap amusing stories.

MEDITATE

Meditation has been used by many cultures around the world for centuries. Yoga and t'ai chi are both described as "moving meditation," which shows that this practice takes many forms. You don't necessarily have to sit cross-legged and chant mantras to meditate, though you can if this is something you find helpful.

Put simply, meditation is a way of quieting your mind and allowing yourself time to be still. A good way to start, if meditation is new to you, is to sit in a comfortable position with a straight back, resting your hands palms-up in your lap. Close your eyes and focus on one of your other senses, such as your hearing. When your mind begins to wander, gently bring it back to your chosen sense. Doing this for five to ten minutes can make a huge difference to your day.

Tip

CREATIVE VISUALIZATION

Creative visualization is a technique practiced by many as a means of literally 'seeing' where you want to be so that you might have a chance of reaching that end goal. It is easy to be put off by the 'what ifs' that a situation might bring to mind, and this is where creative visualization can help. Find a comfortable chair to sit in and relax. Begin by closing your eyes and focusing on the natural rhythm of your breathing. Next, start to build up a picture in your head of how a happier, more content you would look and behave. Where are you? Who is beside you in this happy place? Notice every detail and enjoy how it feels. While you are working on becoming happier with your life, carry this mental image with you as inspiration.

Affirmations

An affirmation is a positive phrase that you use to help change negative beliefs to positive ones. Affirmations work well when written down and when said out loud. A positive affirmation to help you change your attitude to stressful situations could be:

"I feel balanced and happy."

Or:

"I solve my problems quickly and effectively."

It is important that the affirmation focuses on the positive outcome that you want rather than the negative possibility that you wish to avoid, and that it is written or spoken in the present.

PART 3

Achieve a Healthy Work/Life Balance

So many of us live fast-paced lives, dashing from one commitment to the next — be it work, family, social activities, study, etc. — that we constantly feel like we're playing catch-up and our personal needs are ignored. One of the joys of *lagom* is that it encourages a slower pace of life. In this section, we look at how to apply the principles of *lagom* to achieve balance by making space for "me" time and simplifying your life so it's only populated with what's important to you.

Lagom at work

Allow yourself to daydream for a moment and visualize your ideal work scenario, and ask yourself the following questions:

Does it involve working away from home or at home, or would you prefer to divide your time between the two environments?

Would working part-time enable you to work on dream projects?

Would freelancing or flexible working be the way to go?

Do you feel you work too much?

How can you balance work with your values and needs?

Brainstorm your ideas and see how you can match up your work life to your needs. You may decide working less is sensible, but you need to consider living on a tighter budget — in which case, work out a budget for what you can realistically live on and see if you can make it work.

Simplify your work week

Does your day start off with good intentions and a list of items to be fulfilled, only for you to get to the end of the day and find barely anything has been done, because other things have gotten in the way?

Ask yourself these questions:

 Am I taking on too much?

 Am I making the best use of my time?

 Am I happy with the way I'm spending my time?

We are all guilty of taking on too much — often because we are encouraged to challenge ourselves, and have a fear of saying "no" to things and missing out on something important.

The reality is, if you spread your time too thinly, you won't be able to do your best job on the things that are most important to you. It's also likely that you will become stressed and neglect your personal needs.

Take a look at your schedule and highlight the areas that would benefit from more time spent on them, and look into how you could delegate other tasks or find a more efficient way to get them done.

DON'T COMPARE YOURSELF TO ANYONE ELSE

It's common to compare yourself with others, such as considering someone else to have a better job, a bigger house, more money, etc. than you, which steers you away from looking at all the positive things happening in your life. Don't believe that emulating others will make you happy; try to be the best version of you and look at the areas in your life that could be improved upon as well as recognizing and appreciating what you're good at. Whenever you find yourself comparing yourself to someone else who you consider to have "more" of something that you want, or a "better" life, remember the *lagom* principle of not being perfect but "just right" for you. Remind yourself of your achievements and allow yourself to feel good.

Get organized

Being organized involves forward planning, and though it can be hard to get motivated, even to do something simple such as picking out your outfit for the next day when you'd rather go to bed for example, your future self will thank you for it.

- Pick a quiet time on the weekend to go through your work commitments, family activities, etc. for the week ahead so you know what's coming up. Don't get caught unprepared when your child has been invited to a costume party and they're the only one in plain clothes!

- The night before a work day (or "school night" as I still call them!), get your clothes ready for the next day — make sure they're ironed, select accessories and shoes (give these a polish), and you'll find the morning routine a whole lot easier.

- If you have to share a bathroom with others, arrange a time slot so there's no hanging around as you wait to use it. It might sound a little militant, but it will reduce your stress levels.

- As soon as an appointment is made, or a meeting is organized, add it to the schedule, be it an old-school notebook or an online calendar system.

TEN-MINUTE MORNING HACKS

It's amazing how much tidying and decluttering can be done in a few minutes before you begin your working day. These tips are a great way to ease yourself into simplifying your life and getting off to a good start:

- Go through your pile of mail (yes, we all have one) and open everything. Chances are you will be able to discard most of it. If it's mail that has sensitive information — bank details, for example — either shred it or invest in a garden incinerator. File away things you want to keep in a expanding file folder with labeled compartments, such as house, medical, work, children, pets, etc.

- Book all your appointments in one round of phone calls: dentist, optician, doctor, hairdresser, etc.

- Select three of your favorite songs and tidy your workspace while the songs are playing — it's so much easier to work in an uncluttered and attractive environment, and listening to great music will set you up for the day.

Keep it simple when communicating with others

- ● E-mails – Deal with these in batches rather than as they come in. Some people get very impatient if they don't receive a reply within the hour, but don't feel stressed. Go at your own pace; work through one or two items on your to-do list before attending to your e-mails. If you find this hard to do — especially when you see a reminder popping up at the side of your screen — then turn off your e-mails until you are ready to address them.

- ● Meetings – Assess whether a meeting is required to discuss a particular issue, or is it an excuse for a coffee and a chat? A phone call might be enough.

- ● Making a request – Be concise and clear about your requirements and always include a workable deadline. Follow up with an e-mail to clarify the details.

- ● Dealing with difficult people – Try to nip issues in the bud before they escalate. If you experience unpleasant behavior in the workplace, do your best to avoid a confrontation, document the incident, and inform your manager.

be happy

LEARN TO SAY "NO"

We all want to do well at our jobs, but it can be easy to fall into the habit of always accepting work and piling pressure on ourselves. The concept of saying "no" to your superior when they ask you to complete a task can be a daunting one, but it is important not to worry that you will lose their respect if you refuse. Those in charge understand that sometimes our workload does not permit us to take on additional tasks and responsibilities; they rely on their employees to let them know when and if they are able to do more. Politely declining a task with the explanation that you will not be able to complete it in the time needed will not only show your boss that you are aware of your workload and limits, it will also help alleviate your stress. If you always feel you have to say "yes," then you may be left with too much work, and will have the added pressure of finishing tasks late, of not completing them to the desired quality, or of having to work additional hours to complete them. This is easy to avoid; just keep an awareness of what you need to do, and say "no" if you need to.

Going for goals

Lagom is about decluttering your life and focusing on what really matters, and this includes your personal hopes and dreams, and making time to realize them.

BALANCE THINKING VS. DOING

It's a constant internal argument for many — thinking about doing something over actually doing it. It's important to strive for the things we want and going for our goals, but there's only one thing that can stop us: procrastination. Here are the common excuses we tell ourselves:

- "I don't have time to do it."

- "I might fail."

- "If I leave it, someone else can sort it out."

- "What if I succeed and I find I can't cope?"

If it's something you really want to do, don't put it off:
JUST DO IT!

Switching from intention to action is a huge step. Now it's time to get motivated. It can be easier to encourage others in their plans than to motivate ourselves, so getting a support team in place can be a good way of working toward your goals. Maybe you have friends who have plans of their own? You needn't be going for the same goal: One person may be eager to start a new health regime, while someone else may want to change their job or study for a new degree. What matters is that you find a time to meet regularly and update one another on your progress. Even if it's a quick 15-minute chat after work or a coffee on a Saturday morning, you'll come away feeling boosted by their enthusiasm and advice, and they'll feel the same way, too.

Tip

KEEP CHALLENGING YOURSELF

It may take years of patience and determination to master a skill, such as drawing well or learning a foreign language, but studies show that you have a greater chance of being happier day-to-day in the long term if you actively pursue a pastime or course of study. That feeling of losing yourself in study or a creative pursuit is referred to as "flow," and this state, according to some psychologists, is where true contentment lies.

Money

Do you often find that your monthly expenditure outweighs what comes in to your account? Having too little money depends not only on how much you earn but also what you do with it. Analyzing your outgoing funds should highlight areas where you could make savings.

- **Banking charges:** Make sure you have a fee-free account and check it daily to avoid overdrafts.

- **Unused subscriptions:** Do you pay for gym membership and visit less than once a week? If so, cancel your membership and buy the odd day pass or get in shape at home for free.

- **Insurance on appliances:** One policy for all your major appliances can be more cost-effective than paying for separate policies.

- **Luxuries:** We all deserve a treat, but if you're strapped for cash, try reserving meals out for really special occasions or ditching your daily frappe latte.

- **Stay up-to-date:** Pay everything on time and keep your records up-to-date. This way, you'll have the info on hand if you need to dispute anything or fill out any claims.

- **Consolidate your debts:** Pay off debts before siphoning any money into savings — the interest you pay on your debts will far outweigh any savings' income.

- **Stagger annual payments:** Organize them so that they don't all hit your account at the same time. Try to schedule them for a "good" month, when you have fewer expenses.

- **Budget:** Set aside a monthly amount toward costs such as car expenses, dental bills, and pet care.

Tip

Check out price comparison sites to find the best deals on credit cards, car insurance, energy, broadband, etc. It might be tedious but it will save you money in the long run. Make sure you're getting the best deal on your savings and bank accounts, too. Are you entitled to any benefits or assistance?

There are several useful websites that offer independent financial advice and include detailed information on how to check out all of these issues.

Family activities

Are you or your family members doing too many activities? Are you constantly jumping in the car to take one child to one activity, another to the next, then another for you? It can be dizzying to maintain multiple activities and if you're finding it too much, it's time to set some rules. Ask yourself the following questions:

- Are the number of activities a source of stress for you?

- Do all of the activities deserve a place on your calendar?

- What would constitute just the right amount of activities for your family?

If your answer is yes to the first question, write down the list of activities and think about which ones are really important to you. Just as with work reponsibilities, if you have too much to do, you won't be able to allocate the time and energy to the things that are really important. Confer with your family and make a decision to perhaps have no more than one activity per person per week — this might be too little or too much — but compromise is key to managing family time so everyone gets the chance to do the things that are important to them.

Social commitments

This is another situation where you can often feel motivated by guilt or a feeling that if you don't accept an invitation to go out with friends that you might not get asked again, or they might think less of you. But the reality is that they will appreciate your honesty and ability to say "no" to the things that you don't really want to do. Here are some ways to ease your social calendar:

- Distinguish between "should" and "must" in terms of social engagements — if it's a "should" but you'd rather not, then don't be afraid to say "no."

- Stop seeing the people that make you stressed. This can be difficult if it's a family member, but limiting your time with them will help.

- Have a balance of commitments — decide how many is just right, perhaps one social engagement is enough; set aside a particular day each week to meet up with a friend or a group.

TV/screen time

Too much time on an electronic screen or watching TV and too little movement is unhealthy. The average child is believed to spend around seven hours per day on screens, whereas adults spend around ten hours per day. The way to get the family active and away from screens is to install a few healthy practices, such as:

- Keep track of screen time to get a clear picture of how much time you and your family members spend on screens — use an app or simply switch off the wi-fi connection after an hour or two, and make sure the time is well spent — doing homework or catching up with friends, rather than scrolling endlessly through Instagram or Facebook.

- Ease the family into reducing screen time by an hour at first, and gradually reduce it, if you want to avoid all-out war.

- Schedule family time and make sure you're all doing *something* together. It could be as simple as going to the park, walking in the garden, or going to the market — anything that will engage the family for up to an hour. You'll find that these pockets of time together will become special and enjoyable to all of you, even though some might begrudge them at first.

- Try to eat together — we all have to eat and it's the best reason to sit down together and nurture your relationships. Ask direct questions, such as "How was your meeting with x?" or "What was the best part of your day?" and get the conversation flowing. Needless to say, phones and tablets should be a no-no at the table!

Lagom is about clearing the decks and focusing on what's really important, and what can be more important than spending time with the ones you love most?

Tip

Be mindful of media consumption and what you absorb. Think about how watching the news before you go to bed might affect you, for example. Limit your worries and allow yourself to enjoy your last hour before bed by reading a good book or having a conversation with your partner, or calling up a friend and having a good gossip session.

Sleep

The optimum amount of sleep for most adults is between seven and nine hours a night, but everyone is different. The best way to work out how much sleep you need is to listen to your body. Regardless of whether you're meeting the recommended guidelines or not, if you feel rested, you're probably getting enough sleep, and if you constantly feel tired, then that's a clear signal that you're not. Try to have a set time that you go to bed that will give you the ideal amount of sleep every night.

Declutter your mind before bed

One of the most common causes of sleep loss is an overburdened mind. We've all experienced it, some more than others. It's important to learn to pack up your worries before you head to bed. You might find that writing down how you're feeling will help to unburden you — perhaps you could write in a diary or make a to-do list for the next day. You might also find that talking to a friend or family member helps to calm you. The aim is to feel as stress-free as possible before your head hits the pillow.

There is a calmness to a life
lived in gratitude, a quiet joy.

RALPH H. BLUM

Press pause

Life is short and it's important that you factor in time to do the things you enjoy. Schedule some downtime on your calendar each week. If you have wall-to-wall commitments, think about whether you really *have* to do everything on your calendar. Will anyone notice if you take bought items along to a party rather than cooking something yourself? Can you arrange to swap babysitting or other duties with a friend if you agree to return the favor another time? If you have kids, set up a regular appointment with a babysitter, if possible, or introduce an hour of "quiet time" at the end of each school day so that you can all unwind.

Once you've found yourself a regular slot, don't forget to plan what you want to do in that time, otherwise you'll end up drifting around, catching up on the housework or e-mails.

Be grateful for what you have

Start a daily gratitude journal. List all the positive things in your life — from the small things that make you smile, such as the view from your window, to the bigger things, such as your health or your family. At night, list three things you were grateful for during the day and you'll soon start focusing naturally on the positives.

Amazing fun for all the family with cardboard packaging

These activities are not only creative, fun, and free, but they are a wonderful recycling challenge in which all the family can get involved.

MAKE A CARDBOARD FORT! ▷

The humble cardboard box can be made into the stuff of dreams. From pirate ships and cat hotels to fairy-tale castles and double-decker buses — all you need is a little imagination and a lot of cardboard and packing tape! For a pirate ship, like the one pictured, you will need one large cardboard box. Cut the top and one side off the box, so the box has no top and one open side. Use the piece that you have cut off to make the port side by creating a large V-shape and attaching it to the main part of the box with packing tape. Then decorate the outside with portholes and a skull and crossbones. Then, if you have any other cardboard available, create a flag by attaching a piece of card to a piece of garden cane, and finish it off with a piece of cardboard tubing as a telescope.

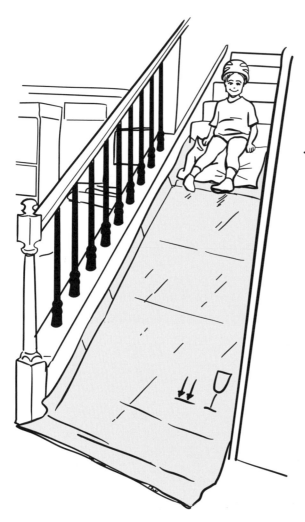

◁ STAIRWAY SLIDE

Use a large cardboard box — the type that houses a new washing machine or dishwasher — to build an amazing stair slide. Here's how: Flatten the box and tape the cardboard to the stair wall using masking tape. Pile pillows and blankets at the bottom to make a soft landing pad and then let the fun begin!

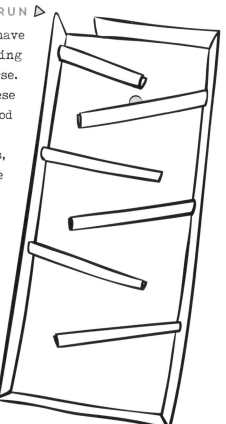

This is possibly the most fun you can have with cardboard tubes — after exhausting them as makeshift lightsabers, of course. There's usually an abundance of these after Christmas, and they're just too good to throw away.

Cut the tubes into three equal lengths, then cut them lengthways, so that you have created a number of chutes. Then apply these to a bulletin board or a thick piece of cardboard, using thumb tacks (for the bulletin board) or a hot glue gun or duct tape (for the cardboard). It's important to place the chutes at gentle inclines and they must overlap each other so that the marbles can travel all the way to the bottom of the course. Get creative and think of different ways to angle the chutes!

PART 4

Balance Your Needs with the Wider World

Thinking *lagom* invites you to consider the needs of the environment as well as that of your local community and beyond. There are a variety of ways that you can do your part and this section offers all kinds of ideas to get you inspired. Just think how different the world would be if we all made one positive change.

Be the change you want to see

Aside from the suggestions in the previous sections of this book on reducing energy, water use, and food waste, etc. here are some easy ways to make a difference.

▷ **LEAVE THE CAR AT HOME**

The next time you need to go somewhere that's less than a couple of miles away, stop yourself from getting in the car and walk or ride your bike there instead. *Lagom* encourages a slower and healthier pace of life, and this is one of the easiest ways to adopt this ethos. Not only will you not be contributing to harmful carbon emissions by leaving the car at home, but you're getting exercise and you're more than likely to bump into people you know, so the social aspect is beneficial, too!

▷ **TAKE A STAYCATION**

Make a promise to vacation closer to home instead of taking a flight. Not only will you significantly reduce your carbon fooprint — return flights from Europe to the United States adds 3–4 tons to your carbon footprint — but you are also likely to save money.

▷ **GO PAPERLESS**

We all receive a lot of mail, but how much of it do we really need? There are simple ways to reduce mail, such as paying bills online, subscribing to online bank statements, and unsubscribing from catalogs. Access books and magazines at a library — the best part is it's free!

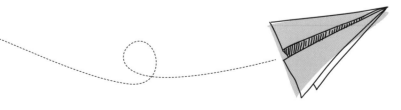

We've all been educated about the effects of plastic on wildlife, especially marine animals.* Here are some simple tips to follow to reduce your impact on plastic use:

- Use reusable fabric shopping bags instead of disposable bags for life.
- Use a reusable bottle, such as a thermos, and a metal lunchbox instead of a plastic one.
- Don't use plastic bags to carry your fruit and vegetables. Try using fabric bags instead.
- Take a set of cutlery to work rather than picking up the disposable plastic ones if you buy lunch from a supermarket.

*If you have a spare day on the weekend, volunteer for an environmental clean-up to see first-hand how much trash washes ashore or is thrown out on the highway.

THINK BEFORE YOU GET TAKE-OUT

Coffee will always be popular, but those paper cups that you have for your to-go coffee end up in a landfill — around 2.5 billion of them, and only one in 400 is recycled.* That's a lot of cups. Do your part by taking a reusable cup and asking the barista to fill it instead of using a disposable one. Some coffee shops will give you a discount for doing this but the idea that you're not adding to the landfill is good enough, right?

*According to Friends of the Earth.

Be kind

Doing things for others is not only a great way to take your mind off your own worries; it also feels good. One recent study concluded that those who volunteer for selfless reasons live longer, and altruism is also linked to stronger and happier relationships.

COMBAT LONELINESS

Help to combat the loneliness epidemic and volunteer to spend time with an older, isolated person in your community via elderhelpers.org. You may have a neighbor that doesn't have many visitors or their family might live too far away to be a regular part of their lives. Offer to do small things for them like weed their garden or do some grocery shopping.

HELP THE HOMELESS

Offer to help at a homeless shelter by making and serving meals, or donate blankets and warm clothes such as coats, wool socks, and sturdy shoes.

BECOME A SPONSOR*

If you want to make a regular donation and have a particular interest, look up ways to donate to a preferred charity or become a sponsor. You could help a female survivor of war by sponsoring a woman to learn skills to support and sustain her family via womenforwomen.org, or sponsor a child refugee to ensure they have adequate food and shelter via savethechildren.org.

*According to research, money *can* buy happiness, but only if you spend it on someone other than yourself. It's a win–win, because not only will you make someone else feel special, but by doing so you'll feel good, too!

SPEAK UP

Your voice counts. If you have a particular concern relating to your community, write and lobby your representatives and urge them to act. Set up online petitions for issues that you feel strongly about. If you have been the victim of sexism, speak out on everydaysexism.com. Frequent small steps can lead to big changes.

Small acts of kindness

A single act of kindness throws out
roots in all directions, and the roots
spring up and make new trees.

AMELIA EARHART

It's the little things that can mean the most, from giving someone a call to surprising someone with a bunch of flowers, and the best part is that doing good things makes you feel good, too! Here's a list of small but important acts of kindness to weave into your everyday life.

- Call a relative or old friend for a good chat.

- Offer your seat to someone on the bus or train.

- Offer a ride to work to a colleague.

- Be patient.

- Give someone a compliment: It will make their day.

- Give flowers or vegetables from your garden or make some cakes for a new neighbor — or even an old neighbor!

- Write a letter — it is so much nicer to receive a letter in the mail instead of e-mail.

- Remember your friends' birthdays — send them a card or take them out for a drink.

- Clean up litter instead of walking past it. People will notice, and hopefully follow suit.

- Tell someone when they've done something well.

- Put out your neighbors' trash cans on trash day.

- Bring your loved ones a drink in bed in the morning.

- Hold the door open for the next person.

- Remind your loved ones how much you love them.

- Bring healthy treats to work for your colleagues — no more cake!

- Loan someone a book or DVD that you think they would like.

- Offer encouragement to someone who is feeling low.

- Be a good listener.

Give a little time

Offering your time is a wonderful way to engage with your community and share your skills and energy. Here are some ways to give back close to home:

VOLUNTEER AT YOUR LOCAL SCHOOL

Children need role models and people who care about their lives and behavior. Whether you read stories to elementary school children, monitor outdoor activities, help out on field trips, offer to be the crossing guard, or spend a Saturday cleaning up the school grounds, your efforts will be recognized and appreciated. Moreover, you can make an investment that will pay off in the future.

HOLD A BAKE SALE OR GARAGE SALE FOR CHARITY

Consider holding a bake sale or garage sale and dedicating the proceeds to a local charity. Almost every household has electronics, furniture, clothes, or equipment that can be donated because they're no longer in use. These items have value and can be recycled to those who will use them again.

HELP OUT AT A COMMUNITY GARDEN

There are community gardens all over the country where you can exercise your green thumb and learn a few tips along the way as well as meeting people with similar interests. Go to communitygarden.org for information.

COACH A SPORTS TEAM OR HELP OUT AT CUB SCOUTS OR GIRL SCOUTS

There are openings in almost every sport in every community for compassionate teachers and volunteer coaches. Check out the official websites, such as girlscouts.org and scouting.org.

There are national sites relating to all different sports. Get started by contacting the Amateur Athletic Union (aausports.org) or your local parks and recreation department.

If bicycling is more your thing, you can join the League of American Bicyclists and help to make the country more bike-friendly. Visit bikeleague.org for more information.

Give someone a hug!

A good hug is one of the quickest ways to boost happiness levels as it encourages the flow of oxytocin, which soothes your nervous system, lowering blood pressure and stress levels. Obviously, it helps to know the person that you are going to hug, as you might provoke a less-than-happy response from hugging strangers!

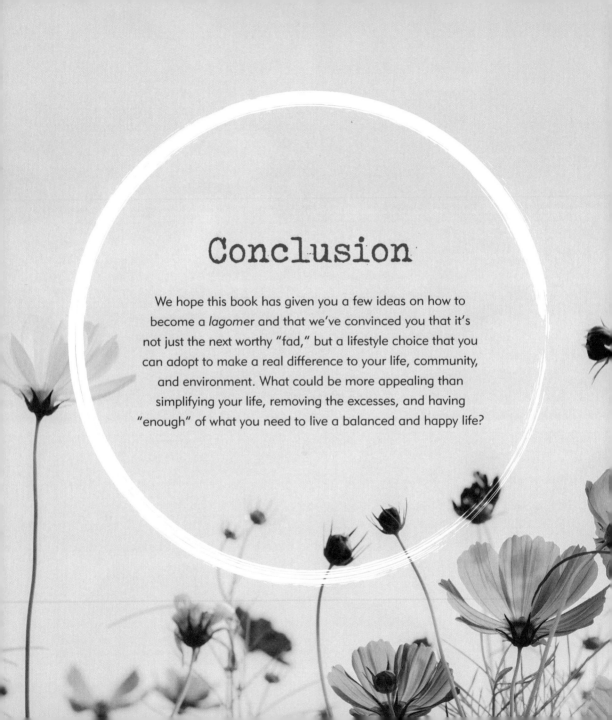

Conclusion

We hope this book has given you a few ideas on how to become a *lagomer* and that we've convinced you that it's not just the next worthy "fad," but a lifestyle choice that you can adopt to make a real difference to your life, community, and environment. What could be more appealing than simplifying your life, removing the excesses, and having "enough" of what you need to live a balanced and happy life?

Resources

THE AMATEUR ATHLETIC UNION

www.aausports.org

A nonprofit, multisport organization promoting the development of physical fitness programs across the country.

AMERICAN COMMUNITY GARDEN ASSOCIATION

www.communitygarden.org

Organization dedicated to supporting community gardens and greening initiatives throughout the U.S. and Canada.

CENTER FOR FOOD SAFETY AND APPLIED NUTRITION

www.fda.gov/food

A branch of the U.S. Food and Drug Administration (FDA) working to keep food safe through consumer education and awareness.

EARTHPARK

www.earthpark.net

Complex of biomes in Des Moines, Iowa; organization promoting environmental awareness.

ENERGY SAVER

www.energy.gov/energysaver

The Department of Energy's online advice portal, offering free guides to make homes and businesses as efficient as possible.

ENVIRONMENTAL PAPER NETWORK

www.environmentalpaper.org

Civil society movement promoting sustainable practices in the pulp and paper industry.

THE FREECYLCE NETWORK

www.freecycle.org

Nonprofit network of people who exchange items for reuse rather than throwing out good stuff into landfills.

FRIENDS OF THE EARTH

www.foe.org

Organization campaigning for sustainable life and preserving the planet.

GLOBAL STEWARDS

www.globalstewards.org

An organization helping people to save energy in everyday life.

GRACE COMMUNICATIONS FOUNDATON

www.gracelinks.org

Promoting consumer actions and public policies to support sustainable food production; awareness of critical environmental and health issues; and a better understanding of the interconnections of food, water, and energy.

HEALTHY PLANET USA

www.healthyplanetus.org

A nonprofit organization that works to inspire a new generation of conscious eaters.

THE LEAGUE OF AMERICAN BICYCLISTS

www.bikeleague.org

U.S. bicycling organization offering programs and resources to promote safe biking throughout the country.

LIVE LAGOM PROJECT IKEA

www.ikea.com/gb/en/ikea/ikea-live-lagom

Project and tips for a more sustainable, healthy, and cost-conscious life at home.

NATIONAL GEOGRAPHIC

www.nationalgeographic.com/environment

The website of the famous magazine offers a whole section dedicated to environment and sustainability.

ONE BROWN PLANET

www.onebrownplanet.com

Their online toolkit offers tips and projects for sustainable living both at home and in the community.

OXFAM

www.oxfamamerica.org

Confederation of charitable organizations working to reduce poverty and injustice; together with Marks & Spencer, they introduced the concept of "shwopping."

PLANET NATURAL

www.planetnatural.com/garden-advice/

Providing expert gardening advice, from herb gardens to composting.

RECYCLE ACROSS AMERICA

www.recycleacrossamerica.org

National recycling campaign, offering simple but effective tips to reduce waste at home.

SURFRIDER FOUNDATION

www.surfrider.org

A community of everyday people protecting the country's seas and beaches.

SUSATAINABLE AMERICA

www.sustainableamerica.org

A nonprofit organization working to make the nation's food and fuel systems more environmentally conscious.

WORLD WILDLIFE FUND (WWF)

www.wwf.org

Independent conservation organization striving for sustainability, reduction of pollution, and better conditions for wildlife.

Sign up:

CUPIFESTO

www.environmentalpaper.eu/cupifesto/

Manifesto of Environmental Paper Network to substitute disposable cups with reusable ones and stop encouraging a throwaway culture.

VOLUNTEER MATCH

www.volunteermatch.org

Bringing people together to help solve society's problems through voluntary and civic action.